Really!

Things Women Know But Refuse To Face

Copyright ©2014 Holloman
ISBN-10:0989727440
ISBN-13:978-0-9897274-4-0
All rights reserved. Printed in the United States of America. No part of this publication may be reproduced, stored in a retrieval system or transmitted in any form or by any means, electronic, mechanical, photocopying, recording or otherwise without the written permission of the author.

This book is dedicated to all precious gems protected by God. Whether you're a top executive or a stripper, an at home mom or a recovering addict, even if you're mentally, spiritually, and physically fit or unhealthy, insecure, and overweight; ladies you're precious to the creator and me so never forget who you are and the purpose only you can fulfill.

Peace and abundant love will forever be with you; just receive it.

Table of Content

Introduction

Do I really love me?

Do I really fear success?

Why am I sleeping with him?

Is it really that hard?

Introduction

Really was inspired by quotes on social media, complaints from men, and topics seen on television; which support conversations heard daily by the women that refuse to stop thinking one dimensional. Some women are celebrating shows where women are fighting, back-biting, and disrespect friends. These shows contaminate the true meaning of friendship or images that don't embrace self-respect and self-love. The images are a small percentage of females, but these images of negativity contaminate the essence of the strong, educated, and productive women that are a positive force in the community and the world. Women are smart, productive, and determined, but some women refuse to acknowledge these things while in relationships

because of the fear of being alone.
This can cause a lack of self-love
and self-respect. Some women
believe there is a piece missing from
their life so it's filled with material
stuff or things of no substance.

Some of the questions that flow
through the minds of women can be:
"I need to drop five more pounds.
"Am I pretty enough?"
"Am I successful?"
"Why won't he marry me?"
The media can control the way some
women see themselves, causing
them to believe they're not whole.
You know the truth; therefore you
look the other way, but some try to
fix a non-existing issue, or fixate on
the perfect fantasy developed within
their minds. Don't fall for the belief
that you're a square peg will not fit
into the round hole when you're
already whole. You're perfect just
the way you were created so don't
concern yourself with trying to fit in.

If you're a person that journals get a new one now. If you're not you need to start, because journaling allows you to see your growth and who you are; if you don't know. Keep track by writing the dates and other info at te top of each page or use several journals for different topics, but don't forget the date. Remember don't beat yourself up because you've missed the mark or haven't seen enough growth because it's coming. Five yourself time because change isn't always easy and neither is accepting you flaws.

My desire is to see women healed, so we can come together in peace without negative thoughts. The strong desire to encourage other women without harsh words behind their back is only obtained thru heathy relationships from healthy women.

Do I really love me?

<u>Do you really love yourself?</u>

Yes, I'm sure was your response. Was there a little neck and eye rolling action? Lol. Now was that an honest answer or the answer that you don't believe yourself? When a person is honest with themselves the person will look at their actions, choices, and thoughts towards themselves for the truth. For some women the demand to become a super everything causes them to question everything she does and this can be toxic. Inviting toxic situations in your life or trying to prove something to everyone else can be a sign of lack within a person's life; which could be a lack of self-love. Appearances tend to dominate a person's life if we allow it to, but always remember you are beautiful in your own uniqueness.

I've started asking the question; "Why?" to some women, so she could hear herself after she responded. If the question was surrounded by validation I knew that could be the root of insecurity or some other underlying issue within a person. Some of the typical questions were:
"I want him to tell me he loves me."
"Why won't he love me like I love him?"

"Why do you believe/think that?" would be my response until the answer comes to her or the revelation of why she asked the question in the first place. Sometimes people brag about the action of love, but need to be validated by words daily. In some cases it's a matter of the persons 'Love Language' so Google the title and get yourself a copy of the book, so you can learn your love language is. Most people say this is just a male or female difference, but I would say it's a respect issue in some cases. In some cases there are circumstances, values, or cultural differences that mingle in the relationship and are adopted. This can change a person's action or attitude. If the issue is more than miscommunication of your love language, there is a bigger issue, so get professional help and remember, ***If you can't or don't love you how can anyone else?*** Understanding your truth is the key so if needed, seek professional assistance and workout knowing you.

What are your actions toward yourself or how often do you,

- Take yourself out to dinner or
- Treat yourself to a movie or
- Love on you the way you want to be loved, not sexual.
  - Send yourself flowers or the things you like
- Be honest with yourself

I hope you can understand where I'm going, so how often do you without being forced,

- Take yourself out just to spend time with you by choice and not circumstances or
- How often do you love on you without saying, "I don't need a man!" or without bashing someone else

Think about it, if you can't spend time with you the next question should be, _"Why would I expect other people to do what I can't do with or for myself?"_

How often are you spending time doing the things you want others to do for or with you? If you can't do the things you want done for yourself, why have an expectation for others to do so? This does not mean you say, "I don't need a man because I can do it for myself." It means that if you know how you want to be treated you can make better choices when meeting someone and expound on what you want in detail. Being accountable for your actions towards you is a step towards loving you without insulting others.

Have you ever said, (*and believed it*)

- ➢ I'm satisfied with who I am today

- I will continue to improve who I am when its negative
- I love me
- I acknowledge all of my imperfections

A person that is secure can strive because their passion encourages them to accomplish the goals set in their plan. When you have healthy thoughts about yourself insecurity can't stop you from striving to do more in your life. Being a kind and productive person allows you to see a positive future for yourself. Detox from negative energy you've released into the atmosphere. Improve what you can about yourself by seeking a life coach or wholeness professional. This doesn't mean something is wrong with you but will help you improve your thought process.

A person that desires joy will achieve natural peace or joy; like a person that craves negativity with their actions or words receives negative results and a lack of positive joy in life. Learning to embrace imperfections will allow a person to understand how to use their strengths and seek others that will complement their weaknesses. Remember just because a negative person appears to be on top doesn't mean it's the reality they live in because insecurity and self-hatred causes them to be negative.

Remember the choices you make today will affect the options you have tomorrow. WAIT! Have you made career plans, financial plans, dating plans, or family plans? If not, get your journal and start today. Remember to be flexible with your plans because life has unexpected changes and a person can't control the world just their actions and thoughts.

Career plans and goals can change as knowledge and wisdom increases, so starting over may be an unforeseen option.

- Start saving and open an IRA the day you get your first paycheck, parents should teach their children and it's not too late for you.

- Dating is a big one because the first question should be, "Why am I dating?" This is a loaded question because everyone has their own definition of why people date, when a person should date, and/or how a person should date; therefore you should Your first goal is to define the why, when, and how for you. This is a question only you can answer; if you're saved seek God not man for the answer. If knowing what you need is not established in the beginning you'll never know when the connection is the right one. I'm not talking about the emotional momentary feel good of sex, this is discussed later. Think about the standard you've set, your lifestyle, and how you want to be treated.

➤ Family plans include the number of children and the basic expenses, and if both parents are going to work or one will stay at home with the children. to rent or own including the location of the home, These are important life decisions and can become difficult when dealing with blended families.

➤ _Seek guidance from a Marriage Therapist or Relationship Consultant before getting engaged or saying, "I do."_

Starting with a plan before a decision is made can be the best asset so when unforeseen obstacles arise you're equipped to handle the obstacles. Life isn't always perfect but you have to make the choice to be okay with whatever issues arise from the choices you make, but don't let issues change you as a person.

Some statements can be unhealthy

- I'm overweight but I love me so it's okay
- I'm too loud
- I don't fit in
- I'm not good enough to be this or that
- I think I'm better than her or anyone else

- I don't need a man because I can do it on my own; from pain
- I have to be in a relationship
- I can't go out and have fun or enjoy myself alone
- I'm the best thing that ever happened to him or her.

The weight issue has and will always be controlled by society's standards. If you have a weight goal let it be your goal not someone else's, this can invite unhealthy thoughts or actions. If you need to drop a few pounds for health reasons don't hesitate, this is an act of self-love. What people think of others or how you view yourself can determine your compassion level. It's unhealthy to compare yourself to another person. That means you are trying to fit in and it can cause a person to see themselves in a negative way. Loving you gives you the power to love others where they are. That doesn't mean you allow people to mistreat you or that you have to like their actions, but respect who they are. The reality is no one is better than anyone. It's just that some people know what they want in life and go after it; while others are confused or lack the self-encouragement to strive for more. There are people that lack exposure so their view of life can be boxed in, but that does not mean it is okay to condemn the person. Everyone will not like you and some will talk about you, but that's not your issue it's theirs. You cannot please everyone so don't try, but remember the feeling you had when someone talked about you before you talk about someone else.

Here are some tips:

- Challenge yourself to improve one negative issue at a time
- Workout daily
    - Build up to it every other day or 5 to 10 minutes a day. Rest twice a week
- Stop worrying about what other people think
- Say a positive affirmation about you daily
- Think about what you are going to say before you speak

That famous line, "I don't need a man," that so many women say. Yet, they curl up in bed alone crying while praying for a man that she said she didn't need in front of her girlfriends. Tearing men down or telling your girlfriend, "If that was me..." when she tells you about the issues within her relationship is negative and unhealthy. The decisions you would make are not relevant let her work out her issues and be an ear of compassion. If your girlfriend gives you advice and she starts out with, "Well girl, if it was me..." run to the nearest exit and don't look back. Keep negative or bias advice out of your relationship and hers. In cases of domestic violence encourage her to seek professional help because things can quickly become escalated. Before giving her advice seek professional assistance.

Most ladies desire a mate so it's time to stop lying to yourself and set boundaries instead of false realities. Set realistic standards which will be a list of things you will and won't accept within a friendship. This also applies when dating, so expound on why you will or won't accept certain things, read the list aloud. When we hear our thoughts we see things differently. The last bullet point on

page 18 could be true, but if a couple is not meant to be together it's irrelevant so move on and the best thing doesn't mean the right thing. I want you to ask yourself why you think you're the best thing that ever happened to him. You could've been the one preparing him for the one he's supposed to be with or vice versa. If one of the reasons is, "I did this and that for him." I'll just say this, <u>*"That was a choice you made."*</u>
Using what you say you did out of love as a reminder to him is proof that you don't understand love. When you love someone you don't keep account of what you've done because you did it out of love. That's unconditional love.

When people see themselves in a positive way their accomplishments in life can multiply. The only way this can be negative is if it means comparing yourself to another person or tearing a person down to build you up. This is an unhealthy thought process. Remember these actions start with a thought before the act is completed or the words flow from the mouth so you make a choice to allow it to die or plant the seed and allow it to grow...

The questions/statements below are some of the keys to your happiness (joy), wholeness, and the peace you have in your life. Once you've accepted the truth you'll understand joy starts with you, so no one can take, steal, or rob you of that internal peace but you. This doesn't mean you won't get upset , make mistakes, or have some off moments because life happens; so don't beat yourself up. You can always pick up where you started. Whether you're married, single, or divorced the basic applications apply (If you're married create a plan with your spouse too). Regardless of a person's age it's never too late to adjust your thought process or increase your understanding of wholeness through peaceful positive thinking.

Do you really love you?

After meditating on the question, write or say your answer aloud; did anything change? Get your journal and start writing. Don't forget to write down the date.

Notes

Is she really your friend, so...

...is she?

Now ask yourself, *"Are you really her friend?"*

Often women are not honest with themselves about relationships. Because some women have examples of poor behavior by past generations or societal norms have been adapted so there can be a distorted understanding of what being a friend is. Women have been subconsciously conditioned to tear other women down; therefore being allies against the world to encourage others is not the goal. When we look at reality shows where friends talk behind each other's back, yet say they're friends is confusing.

If you're a friend answer these questions:

- What is your definition of a friend?
- Would you be friends with someone doing some of the things you do to the people you call friend?

In some cases the reality of true friendship has been contaminated so we must break those generational curses. This doesn't apply to all women because not all women partake in this behavior so the questions you need to ask yourself would be:

- "Can she trust me?"
- "Do I talk behind her back?"
- "Do I keep her secrets?"
- "Can she depend on me?"

This is a matter of trust within a person's character because a friend is someone that should trust their friend. The problem is some people in society have become selfish momentary pleasers of themselves. Their only concern is what fulfillment they will get out of the situation or acceptance that comes with this betrayal. If you're a Christian this should never be because pleasers of themselves to get praises from man can infect the Church; therefore the lack of love prevails. A friend should accept their friend unless they display negative behavior; therefore correcting the negative actions of a friend is acceptable but not through gossip with others. Trust is a beautiful gift that should never be tarnished. You are responsible for your actions within the friendship so if you don't feel as if you can be a friend let her/him know. Honesty is a rare quality within some relationships. Some people want to protect their own selfish needs but say it's to protect their friend. If you think you're protecting someone by not being honest, you've taken away their right to make a well informed decision so that's selfish not love or respect.

The next set of questions allows you to reflect on your insecurities and level of jealousy.

- "Am I okay with her having successful relationships?"
- "Do I think I would be a better mate for her boyfriend or husband?"
- "Can I trust her with my deepest secrets?"
- "Can I trust her alone with my mate?"

Some women can't handle their friends having successful

relationships so they become jealous and try to sabotage the relationship. If you are always joking about being a better mate for him; you have issues. Ladies reevaluate your friendship if your girlfriend is doing that. If you're doing it you must be honest with yourself. I suggest seeking professional help if you can't control yourself.

   If you can't trust her with your secrets or depend on her you need to walk away from that friendship. If you can't trust her with your mate/boyfriend check yourself to understand why you have these feelings. If he's a cheater ask yourself why you're still in a relationship that breeds insecurities. If she's that type of person why are you still friends or why haven't you advised your friend to seek professional help for unhealthy behavior?

Is she your friend or a succubus? *A 'succubus is a demon that has sex with men drawing energy out of them',* but I change definition. I became friends with this person but after seeing her mess over several people until she was sustained I change the definition. After viewing her actions I decided to call people that sucked the energy/life from others for their own selfish needs a succubus.

These are the questions I started asking after my own experiences.

- Can I depend on her?
- Am I drained every time I talk to her?
- Am I always paying for her and if so is it by choice, unforeseen force, or circumstances?
- Am I gossiping

If you're the one that's always there for them, but they can't find the time to support or be there for you it's time to reevaluate your relationship. Ask them why and seek resolution before making a final decision. If you're drained or lack energy after talking to your friend it's time to reevaluate the relationship and encourage them to seek professional help. Examine your motives before making a decision. You pay for everything because this person is cheap then reevaluate the relationship to ensure they are not using you. If they are always in a financial struggle because of life choices, then as a friend it's your choice to treat them and love them where they are. If you complain behind their back you're not a friend and can't be trusted because you had an option to say no and tell your friend why. Point them towards professional help.

If you're around a person that continually gossips about others or criticizes other's character and physical appearance, this can be a sign of an insecure person. Suggest the person seek professional help. It's a struggle to accept the truth about yourself and just as difficult to reveal the ugliness in someone close to you. It's time to reevaluate yourself, your friends, and your atmosphere.

➢ Is your atmosphere, negative or positive
➢ Are you honest about your feelings, thoughts, or actions

These questions should only be used for platonic relationships, so be honest. Are you surprised by your answers or have you thought about these questions before today?

Being a friend is more than just saying the words but through a person's actions the truth is revealed. I know one of the things I said was being able to keep secrets, but if the secret is harmful to their family, illegal, or their health let them know you can't keep that secret but you will be a shoulder if they need you. One secret could be they are cheating on their spouse. I don't believe that a friend would let their friends dwell in unhealthy relationships or issues. Being a friend means I can call you at three in the morning for a ride home, but it also means I love you enough to respect you and your mate so I would not put the relationship in a toxic or unnecessary situation.

So is she really your friend?

<u>Are you her friend?</u>

Are you sure, why do you believe you are? Write it in your journal.

Notes

Do I really fear success?

Do you fear success?

The fear of success is not just in career goals, but it can be relational, personal goals, or with family. There are people that self-sabotage or can be their own worst enemy; because of fear. Fear is not always recognized as the issue, but it can be the source. Why, because fear can be uncontrollable for some since stepping out of your comfort zone is not a natural act for most individuals. Fear may not always be conquered, but it can be controlled. Most people like the comfort of habits just as much as an adventurer loves the excitement of the unknown. People can experience fear in different forms at any time, so the comfort of repetition is a false assurance that everything will be the alright.

What are your plans for success?

- ➤ What are your daily, weekly, monthly, or yearly goals
- ➤ Have you created measurable goals with milestone celebrations
- ➤ Have you created particular career, family, dream and or vacation goals (Why)
- ➤ What motivates you to follow or stay focused on your goals
- ➤ Have you done any research on your goals, dreams, or desires
- ➤ Don't forget about a Financial Planner, Life Insurance,

Prepaid Funeral plans, Living Will or Will plans, and etc.

There are some things that can't wait because life happens and will continue to go on, so don't let it throw you off. The best thing to do is get a Financial Planner or someone that specializes in your particular needs. If you don't have a lot of money you can do the research yourself, go to the library for books, attend free seminars, or use the internet to assist you. Start planning for your retirement and saving for a rainy day now or plan your vacations early so you can get bargains. Another great idea is to learn how to live off one paycheck; if you're married. Invest time in a success or accountability partner; if you're married become each other's accountability partner. Seek outside help if this causes issues.

These are just a few suggestions to overcome the fear of success as you plan for life's obstacles. Refer to a professional because I'm just giving suggestions. I am not a certified Financial Planner or Life Coach.

Notes

Do I really need this?

Sometimes we buy things to fill the gaps in our lives to avoid the fear factor of success. I look the part so that's enough. _Wrong_. These purchases can be things to impress others, or items that allow you to keep up with the Jones's. The things you do that makes you feel accomplished can be unhealthy. I'm not saying you shouldn't buy things that you love or make you happy, but you must ask yourself why you're buying these things.

I'm a shoe girl so in some circles I'm known for and I've even been introduced by my shoes. The owner of my favorite accessories and shoe store told me I had a shopping issue. I didn't know how to receive the information so I defended my actions. I am a person that hates to shop, but I will buy shoes all day long, so I couldn't grasp that truth. At this time I was buying more than shoes. After meditating on the statement I realized why I was spending money recklessly. I was unemployed and depressed, so I bought shoes and clothes; which were on sale, to make me feel better. I don't buy a lot of clothes, but I was buying them as well. I bought more shoes than usual so they just sat in my closet. That was money wasted because I could have done something productive with the money. My friend alerted me to my actions. We can all get depressed in life because of circumstances but if it last more than a few days seek professional help. I'm not saying shopping is a sign of depression but why you're doing certain things can be a warning sign. Depression can display in many forms, so recognize a change in your actions.

Do you really need that?

This question isn't just about shopping, but can include food, men, extra sleep, and or taking days off work to name a few. Has anything changed in your life that will cause different circumstances?

Avoidance relationships are toxic because they are used as distractions to avoid reality and fear of being alone. Listed are a few possible fear based avoidance relationships?

- ➤ Sleeping with a person because you don't have to focus on what's going on around you
- ➤ Dating a guy you know is unhealthy for you because you don't want to be alone

- Being in or a part of anything that takes you away from reality or your issues
- Starting arguments to avoid the truth

Enjoying yourself while single is healthy but having a sexual relationship with a man because you don't want to face life alone or be lonely is unhealthy. Being lonely is a state of mind so if you dwell on being lonely or alone it becomes your reality. Whatever takes you away from reality and into a false reality is unhealthy. Never avoid the truth even if it hurts because of the harmful side effects. Once you've faced the truth don't allow anyone to use it to hurt you or hold it over your head. Release negative people from your close circles, but always respect and be cordial to them.

There are also things you shouldn't do because you are avoiding the truth, or fear facing reality because you're single:

- Becoming a see-food eater to avoid negative feelings
- Staying in a unhealthy relationship
- Lying to your girlfriends about why you're not going out since you don't have any money

Never allow your feelings to determine your actions. Be honest to yourself and with those around you.

Sometimes we know the latest gossip, reality show updates, or what's happening on our favorite drama but lack the knowledge of financial planning for the future, home buying, or wills to protect our assets/estate (everything you have is valuable but if you don't think remove it from your space). What is your value, do you have a retirement plan, savings for a hardship, or investments? Are you still trying to satisfy a momentary feeling instead of facing reality?

Those are some of the tools you can use to focus on being successful in your journey.

Notes

Notes

Why am I really sleeping with him?

This is a popular question between some girlfriends or a silent thought that has gone through a woman's mind, but some women refuse to accept the answer or avoid the truth. Some women have sex out of obligation, insurance to get the ring or to keep a man; while feeling empty inside. If you're having sex to get or keep a man you're headed for heartbreak, confusion, and an increase of unnecessary baggage. Some women must understand their baggage was created by the person in the mirror not your ex.

"Is it okay to have sex?" I've been asked this question several times by women. My reply will always be the same which is,

"Can you handle the consequences of your actions? When the relationship doesn't work out or if he is having sex and dating other women, will emotions control your actions?"

Ladies if you can't handle the emotional baggage that comes along with a sexual relationship you should not go forth in one. Women are not created to think, act, or do what men do; therefore most women can't handle the emotional ties or soul ties. These ties come with a sexual relationship so why get into an emotional hole if you can avoid it? Most ladies can't just have a sexual relationship because it's unnatural to our natural make-up or DNA to nurture, so be honest with you.

Women are natural nurtures so the closeness of a sexual relationship penetrates their heart because, in some cases, their mind has already created a fairytale reality of how things will be between her and the man. Some ladies are not emotionally equipped to do what some men do because women were created different. Your choices dictate the results of your outcome so take responsibility for your actions. Ladies, it's time to stop blaming men for your poor choices and the things your knew, but didn't want to accept for what it was.

If you are having sex with a man that says, "I don't want a committed relationship." Believe him and leave him alone or stop having sex with him if you want a relationship because he may not give you what you want. **Sex does not change his mind.** Don't get upset or start having freaky sex with him because you think it's going to change his mind. He was honest and we must respect the lost quality. Date him without giving it up; too see if he's worth your time or your body. The time frame on when to have sex or the decision to have sex or not to have sex should be yours ***ALONE*** not mine or anybody else's. If you make a choice to have sex you can't blame him for tricking you. ***DON'T*** have unprotected sex or get pregnant so you can keep a man; you could be the only one carrying the baggage of your choices, whether it's a child or incurable STD.

Let's look at these questions. <u>**Use the journal to take notes.**</u>

- ➢ Why are you with him
- ➢ Do you see a future with him
- ➢ Are you trying to change him
- ➢ Are you trying to fix him

> How much of yourself have you given up to be with him
> Does he really have the friend, husband, or father potential that you desire or need

Ladies, it's time to stop looking for absolutes or validation in your relationships by selling yourself short or giving him power over you; while blaming him for your misery. Let me say this, "<u>ALL MEN ARE NOT DOGS!!</u>"
Why, because people can only do what you allow them to do.

> If he's a dog, what are you or what have you accepted during the relationship for him to believe that it is okay to treat you in a negative way?

- Why should he respect you if you lack the ability to respect yourself?

We must look at ourselves first, not to blame but to acknowledge what we missed or accepted during the relationship.

What are you really doing?

- It's okay if he's not the one and only wants to be friends
- Stop holding on to what was good during the first few dates to justify being with him
    - you know it should be over so move on
- Just because you worked hard to mold him doesn't mean you're supposed to be with him
    - that was your choice

- You don't want another woman to reap the benefits of your labor
    - wake up he's not property
- You refuse to accept the fact you're just a jump off
    - love you first with honesty
- You don't want to be alone
- You feel like you've put in too much work to let another woman reap the benefits
    - <u>Had to be said twice</u>
- He said, "God said you were my wife." Yet everything you've become goes against the word of God

This is why you should be careful when deciding to have sex with someone. So, **"Why are you sleeping with him?"** Be honest and start working on you.

Sex is not the key to get him to marry you so don't go ever go there. I know women in the church are always encouraging marriage, but if you're not ready to be a wife don't let them force their ideals or desperation upon you. Going to the alter is easy, but sustaining a forever after take sacrifice (marriage). If you're not ready to relinquish an independent attitude and submit to the authority that both of you have set for marriage leave it alone and focus on you.

Stop buying into your false reality while in a relationship with a man that only wants to be friends with benefits. When you allow benefits without definitive expectations don't create your own false reality. Stop giving husband benefits to undeserving men that incapable of hold the title. If you're sharing your benefits and become emotionally attached, remove yourself from the situation before it's too late. The longer you wait the more difficult it will be to separate yourself from the situation. Being honest with you is always the best option. It's okay if he only wants to be friends because everyone isn't meant to be together. Your feelings don't mean you're flawed or that something is wrong with you. Falling in love with a man doesn't make you stupid, it makes you human. If you're in a toxic situation and stay the fault is yours not his because you can't force your reality or desires on him.

How many times have you heard the following:
"But he was good to me at first he's just..."
Stop holding on to a one time great past act or the good times of a relationship because it can be

detrimental to your health and wellbeing. If he is physically abusive, seek ***professional help NOW***.

If a man mistreats you and you allow him to continue, you are telling him it's okay to mistreat you. Mistreatment can be cheating, mental or physical abuse, neglecting your feelings, or ignoring your emotional needs. When you know the relationship is emotionally over for him let go and don't force something that's not there. You know it's over so move on. If he wants more he won't let you go.

<u>Don't Play Games</u>

Saying, "I made him the man he is." or "I've put too much time, money and energy into him to let another woman reap the benefits of my work." A man is not a project. The time, money, or energy you gave was a choice not a requirement. If you're not engaged or married stop trying to buy or invest your time with him. This can lead to heartbreak because if he changes his mind you might not be what he wants anymore. This can happen even if you're married or engaged, so seek professional help for your issues. If you need a project to work on become your own project or become a mentor for a low income child.

There are many reasons why women stay in an unhealthy relationship but only you can answer why you stay in yours.

Why are you with him?

Notes

Notes

Does he really want me?

Do you want me?

Most of the time a woman knows the answer, but wants him to answer the question. The answer is obvious or in the back of your mind, so, *"Why are you asking the question?"* Be honest with yourself and accept the truth. There are several reasons we question ourselves when it comes to a mate. We should evaluate why we're asking questions before we question our mate. The reasons can stem from several things like:

> ➢ Desiring to have what someone else has in their relationship

- Comparing what you have in a relationship to what the world or media says it should be or look like
- Insecurities within you or the relationship that cause you to question him
- Because of what your friends or mother says
- Refuse to accept who you are in the relationship

If he wants you it should be obvious. It will not only be in his words but you will see it in his actions. Ladies it's time to stop being fooled by words that don't line up with a person's actions. Women need to see, value, and embrace the actions of love in the not so obvious moments during our relationship, as well as the obvious. Sometimes we buy into our own false reality and try to force it to be true or we will say God ordained it. You know God didn't tell you to take that man, so stop it. Get out of your feelings when making important decisions and forcing God into your lie.

Are you comparing your relationship to books, movies or your parents? If so, **STOP**. Your relationship is your relationship. The boundaries set and the interactions between the two of you will be different than the fantasies you've read about or seen on the big screen. When people allow outside entities determine their actions within their relationship these allowances cause issues between the two people in the relationship.

If you are insecure that insecurity can leaked into your relationship and destroy it. Insecurity is destructive when allowed to invade a person's thoughts. If you're calling him all day or thinks he's cheating because he's not answering his phone or if he's out with friends your relationship is unhealthy. He may want you, but are you pushing him away with your behavior. If a man doesn't love you like you want him to some women think he doesn't want them. Ask yourself:

- ➢ What are you doing to push him away

- ➢ Is it just you imagination

- ➢ Why won't you accept that he does want you

What do you really want from your relationship?

Notes

Notes

Are you the side chick

A female can only be a side chick, mistress, or the home wreaker's accomplice if a man is married. If you're dating a man has a right; as well as you, to date other people because that's the purpose of dating. Just because you decide to play house by living together you're shacking not married, so there is not an obligation from a woman. The man owes you the respect to stay faithful. Keeping other women out of your relationship is his responsibility. I'm not saying it is okay, but if that man sees your value you would be his wife or he would respect you enough not to cheat. This doesn't excuse the woman but she doesn't owe you anything because she has her own issues. If she's dealing with a man that will cheat on the woman he says he loves then he has issues too.

Now are you dealing with a married man?

If so...why? I'm not going to call you all the derogatory names people give the other woman because I have compassion for you. Some women make a choice to get involved with a married man and regret their actions. These ladies could've been in a slump or venerable. Yes, some married men seek out opportunities or desperate women. These ladies allow those moments to dictate their life and decided to believe the lie he told her. In some cases the married man pursues a woman for momentary pleasure or a fantasy, so do not get comfortable with a married man and you'll avoid these issues. Getting comfortable seems harmless, but because of human nature unhealthy bonds can grow. When this happens either party is venerable a forbidden relationship can develop. Being comfortable isn't sexual, but starts with conversation, grows with inappropriate jokes or conversation. This grows with playful touching and sexual conversations before planning secret rendezvous. Use caution because innocent flirting and conversations can lead to extramarital affairs. This is for married women as well.

I've met women that are so caught up with a married man these women have had family's with him or he leaves the wife for the lady. Both situations can be dysfunctional not only for the adults, but the children.

There are some women that seek out married men for fun and uncommitted relationships. These women don't care about anyone or anything but the benefits reaped from theses adulterous relations. They know the rules and their role. They abide by all the rules until they see their meal ticket vanishing without having another one in place.

If you're a side chick seek professional guidance. There could be underlying issues you're dealing with so you can't see your self-worth and the dysfunctional lifestyle you're living. If you choose to be second in his life you must remember you're just something he's doing for the moment and what he did with you he might do to you, so there's no future. Here are some rules that you must abide by as the other woman:

- ➤ Respect his wife
- ➤ Don't call or show yourself to his wife
- ➤ Protect his wife from embarrassment
- ➤ Always use protection
- ➤ If you get pregnant that's on you , so don't involve his wife

- Don't have any expectations
- Don't try to position yourself in his life
- Always remember your place
- Don't involve his friends or family in your mess
- Don't get upset if he doesn't have time for you
- **<u>Seek professional assistance</u>**
- **<u>Stop</u>** being the other woman

To avoid an avoidable situation don't get comfortable with a coworker, church member, or a friend's husband. Even if he's your friend, you must change your comfort level, even if it's to give comfort to the wife.

Notes

Notes

Is it really that hard?

<u>No its not</u>

I've met women who've knowing dated a man that's homosexual yet have the misconception that they can change him. Knock knock, that's reality waking you up. Even though this is rare, it happens. That's no different than a woman dating women because she's been hurt by men. The latter is crazy to me because you knew those guys were unhealthy for you before you laid up with them, moved them in, or gave him a child and the benefits of a husband. It's not fair to the woman you're using to hide your pain in so seek professional counseling before entering another relationship.

We make life harder by not accepting responsibility for our actions and choices. Life isn't hard, but we will have obstacles and challenges. When we blame everyone else for our choices we never accept our share of the issues so growth can never happen. It's time for women to come together;

We should

- Set boundaries on how we will be treated
- Change how we treat each other
- Become a support system for our friends
- Stop gossiping
- Admit when were wrong
- Stop comparing ourselves to other women

- Stop holding him hostage because of what your girlfriends or mother says
- Stop desiring to have what someone else has in their relationship
- Refusing to admit when you're wrong, so you'll start confusion or an argument to hide your wrong or guilt
- Stop trying to keep up with the Jones's
- Embrace our singleness
- Seek counseling before entering into another relationship
    - give yourself time to heal
- Comparing what you have in a relationship to what the

> world or media says it should
> be or look like

We also make it hard when we try to make unavailable men a husband. Let's define an unavailable man for the sake of this topic and yes he can be a married man, but we've dealt with that already. An unavailable man is a man that can't commit emotionally, spiritually, faithfully, or legally separated. Sometimes women make life harder than it needs to be because of their own personal issues or the inability to commit. We always think it's just men but so women are unavailable, but refuse to accept the truth. If you have childhood issue that cause you to be insecure or emotionally unavailable seek professional help.

If the man you're with isn't ready for relationship because he is still legally married move on. This is also the same advice for all unavailable men, so don't waste your time or body. You'll know after two or three date and in-between phone calls what type of person he is, so don't be afraid to ask questions. Always test his actions to his responses. If something isn't adding up take notes because he could be having an off day or moment, don't take a one-time action as a person's true character. People will allow you to meet a representative of them before you meet the real McCoy, so don't be fooled. Allow him to meet you and not a representative. I know everyone plays games but that is what we are trying to eliminate as empowered women.

It's time to stop creating issues that causes life harder than it already is.

Notes

What do I really want in my relationship?

I've heard women say they want a man that has a car, no kids, a degree, or owns his own home before they will date him. I would like for these women to see what they have to offer. If you can't offer or have the same expectations for you think hard about your deal breaker. If you have kids and say a man with kids is a deal breaker, that's okay. If you meet a man that doesn't want kids don't get upset because like you he has a right to make that choice. When you make your decisions be realistic and honest with yourself. Give your top five wants and deal breakers. After that choose the top two deal breakers that you can live with. Then give the top two things you want. Your list should focus on a person's overall personal characteristics but if all you care about is his physical appearance that's your choice. Remember your choices determine you options in the future. Your list can change as you grow so write it in pencil.

<u>Notes</u>

What do you want?

Make a list of deal breakers, what you want in a relationship, what you desire in a man.

Notes

Notes

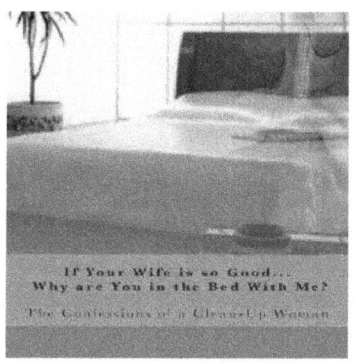

If Your Wife Is So Good...

Follows a woman refusing to accept or acknowledge the pain she's carried from childhood. She seeks out unavailable men for brief flings to protect her heart. The only issue is that the men are good so her flings linger. Alisha finally meets the man of her dreams. She falls in love which causes confusion in her strangely comfortable lifestyle. Alisha chronicles her exploits with an array of unavailable men, as she searches for the one who will make her heart leap. Throughout her journey Alisha struggles with her physical desires for men versus her faith and morals.

www.ingramcontent.com/pod-product-compliance
Lightning Source LLC
Chambersburg PA
CBHW032005060426
42449CB00031B/505